Crab in t...

By Liza Charlesworth

ISBN: 978-1-339-02682-4

Art Director: Tannaz Fassihi; Designer: Tanya Chernyak
Photos ©: p4: Tarpan/Shutterstock.com. All other photos © Getty Images.
Copyright © Liza Charlesworth. All rights reserved. Published by Scholastic Inc.

3 4 5 6 7 8 9 10   68   32 31 30 29 28 27 26 25 24

Printed in Jiaxing, China. First printing, August 2023.

The crab is in the sand.
It's big and red.

The crab is on the man's hand.
It's tan and flat. A crab can
grip stuff.

plants   krill

A crab has ten long legs.
It dips in the sea to grab
plants and krill. Gulp!

A crab can slip in a crack.

It can stand on a rock.

Is a crab quick? Yes!
It can run fast on land.
Zip, zip, zip!

A crab can lay a lot of eggs.
Eggs and eggs and eggs!

What is in the eggs?
Crabs and crabs and crabs!